THE
Archive Photographs
SERIES

EASINGTON LANE

Around the Brickgarth about half a mile,
They won the race in professional style.

Welfare week in Easington Lane, 1962. This was a week of sports and games organised by the Colliery Welfare committee. The pram race was won by Mrs M. Wilson with Mrs R. Sanderson the passenger. This was the Elemore Ladies Club entry.

THE
Archive Photographs
SERIES

EASINGTON LANE

Compiled by
J.R. Sanderson

CHALFORD

The Chalford Publishing Company
St Mary's Mill, Chalford,
Stroud, Gloucestershire, GL6 8NX

ISBN 0 7524 0793 7

Typesetting and origination by
The Chalford Publishing Company
Printed in Great Britain by
Redwood Books, Trowbridge

The author would like to thank everyone who over the years
has provided photographs and information on the history of
Easington Lane.

This was a friendly pub,
If you had no money you could have a sub.
Albion Hotel, 1923. It was known locally as the Monkey House due to the landlord keeping a pet monkey in the bar. The building stood in the High Street opposite the Free Gardeners Arms where the doctor's surgery now stands. It closed around 1935.

Contents

The Four Lane Ends of years long past,
But this scene was not to last.
Four Lane Ends, 1950.

Introduction

The year Eighteen hundred, a farm or two a leafy road,
That was Easington Lane, our abode.
The coal mine of Elemore sunk in 1825,
Then suddenly our village became quite alive.
Houses sprang up around the pit head,
Shops were built our village spread.
But living was rough, and houses were poor,
Labour was cheap, and work never sure.
Gypsies settled in Murton Lane, Tinkers also came,
The Lane was rough, and got a bad name.
Drunkenness, gambling and swearing, became a common sight,
When pubs turned out, there was always a fight.
Churches and chapels were built, these helped a lot,
But still the village, remained a black spot.
Then schools were built, and some education started,
And some of the roughness slowly departed.
Reading classes for adults, in the old reading room,
The old and the young, were invited to come.
December, 2 1886, became a very black day,
Twenty-eight bodies from the Elemore explosion carried away.
But life carried on, new transport did start,
The motor car took its place with the cart.
Then alas in 1914 the Great War started,
Lads from our village to war, departed.
Many never returned, killed in lands far away,
In their memory a Clock Tower stands today.
The twenties and thirties passed with progress slow,
Few new buildings, not much to show.
Then heroes' names on our Clock we had to inscribe,
At the end of the war of '39 to '45.
The forties and fifties saw changes galore,
Old colliery houses were knocked to the floor.
Council estates were built all over the Lane,
Folk would not go back to hovels again.
Now in the late nineties lets look at our lot,
The Lane is no longer a black spot.
Cars stand at many a working man's door,
Lovely carpets adorn almost everyone's floor.
Television sets stand in most sitting rooms,
Electric cleaners in place of the brooms.
But remember those changes took vigour and pep,
To march with the times, and always in step.

Happy carefree camping days,
Where in the sun you could laze.
Independent chapel youth club camping at Darlington in 1945.

Some News of Yesteryear

The first mineral railway in the world was opened on 18 September 1822. It ran from Elemore Colliery to Sunderland Docks. It closed September 1959. Alice Thompson, the oldest person to ever live in the village, died in 1842. She was 105 years of age when she died. Easington Lane's Workmen's Club affiliated to the Club Union in 1912. The villages' Catholic church was built in 1920. The first curate was Father Lucey. Mr and Mrs Linsley were Easington Lane's first council house tenants in 1921. They lived in South Hetton Road. When Easington Lane School opened in 1928 there were 364 children on the roll. The school started the distribution of milk in October 1934. Some children received free milk while other had to pay ½ penny a bottle. Snow drifts closed Elemore Colliery for two days in 1941 with some of the drifts 14 ft deep. In the same year, during heavy snow, only one boy turned up for school. He was sent home. German war planes dropped incendiary bombs on Easington Lane, 11 March 1943. There was no damage reported. The head teacher of Easington Lane School, Miss I.M. Graham was killed in a railway accident when returning home from holiday, 27 October 1947. Snow drifts closed Elemore Colliery in 1947. Workmen with shovels were employed to clear snow away from the engine sidings and colliery railway. Some of them were even sent to the Copt Hill section of the line to clear that area. Robbers stole £2,500 from Easington Lane post office, Februray 1974. Free butter and cheese were given to the old and the unemployed in March 1987. The food came from Common Market surplus. Gale force winds of up to 100 miles per hour caused wide spread damage in March 1990. Easington Lane's largest family, the Wilsons, had 22 children. Two council houses had to be used to accommodate them.

One

Around the Village

Pringles store in Coronation year,
Their store display caused quite a stir.
Pringles store all dressed up for the coronation of George VI, 1937.

The Silver Jubilee of 1935,
You felt happy to be alive.
Pringles store decorated for the Silver Jubilee of George V.

Pringles staff knew their work,
To serve your needs they wouldn't shirk.
Pringles store staff, 1936.

Pringles for butter, bacon and tea,
This was the store in forty-three.
Left to right: N. Fishburn, E. Young, P. Wild, S. Turner, I. Brown, D. Young.

They welcomed you with a smile,
That was the Pringles style.
Two of Pringles staff, John Tonks and Peggy
Wild, 1938.

The wage of shop workers was very poor,
But work was light and very sure.
Pringles staff, G. Bousfield, P. Wild, 1938.

With horse and cart he sold his wares,
In streets he would shout Apples and Pears.
Hudson the fruiterer, 1927. Left to right: two young girls called Pattie, Mr C. Hudson, Mrs C. Carr, Mr J. Hudson, Mrs W. Hudson, Mr Joe Hudson, Mrs Surtees, Mr Carr.

Go in this shop and without a frown,
He would fill your basket for a half a crown.
The fruit shop of Mr J. Hudson, 1929. Left to right: Mrs C. Hudson, Dick Stoker, Mrs C. Carr.

These men would cobble your shoe,
Or make you a pair brand new.
Cobblers shop in Easington Lane, 1900. This shop stood near the top of Pembertons Bank, next door to the Lord Seaham inn.

Kay the butcher for your meat,
One of the best on the High Street.
Kay's butcher shop, 1920.

High Street West, Easington Lane. 5206

High Street looking west,
Anyone was a welcome guest.
High Street houses, 1934. These were pulled down in the 1950s and replaced by council housing.

Nearly completed our Memorial Tower,
A clock was inserted to tell the hour.
The building of the Memorial Tower in 1921 in memory of those killed in the First World War. The stone used in its building was taken from the demolished Mansion House of Hetton Hall. The Robson family from Easington Lane did a lot of the building work and the Tower was unveiled with great ceremony by Lord Joicey on 27 August 1921. The dedication was by Bishop Welldon of Durham, Elemore male voice choir sang the hymns and the music was played by the Murton prize band. It was suitably inscribed with the names of the Easington Lane men who were killed in the war. In later years the names of those killed in the Second World War were added. The building behind the Tower is the old colliery school, which later became the Church Hall when the school closed in 1928. As a matter of interest note the electric tram car on the right. They ran through the village to Sunderland from 1905 to 1925. Trams were available every fifteen minutes and cost one penny a mile.

Names on the Clock recall the wars,
185 died for that bloody cause.
Church Hall and Memorial Tower, 1930.

BANK TOP. EAST⁰ LANE

On Pembertons Bank silent films were shown,
Where now green grass is grown.
On the left side of the road is the old Church Hall and the houses above were on what was called the quay. The building on the second right was the Star Electric Cinema, where only silent films were shown. Later it became the church of the Salvation Army. Note the cobbled road of the bank in 1930.

A little bit of history this picture shows,
Where have the years gone no one knows.
In this street were Wylies hardware shop, Hayes the butcher, and Bousfield the cobbler.

Send for the doctor to treat your ills,
This is how he would arrive with his bag and pills.
This was the horse and rig of Dr Parker a physician in Easington Lane in 1900. The coachman was Mr Tot Stephenson.

Long before the car was king,
Horse and cart was the thing.
Outside the old Gypsy yard in Murton Lane, 1910. The Gypsy yard was an area set aside for the many travelling gypsies and tinkers that would stop or winter in the village every year. In the early 1930s this annual custom slowly declined until it stopped altogether, and the Gypsy yard survived in name only and the area is now a housing estate behind the Workmen's club. Of all the travelling tinkers the only one to settle in the village was Francis the tinner. He was well known for making pots and pans and specialised in miners' water bottles. His descendents still live in the village today.

No worry about crossing the road,
Not enough traffic for a highway code.
High Street, 1906.

A scene of days gone by,
Look close as back in time you fly.
High Street, Easington Lane looking south, 1902. At this time the village boasted fifteen public houses, one corn mill, two schools, seven places of worship, two blacksmiths, one nail factory, one candle factory, three farms and Elemore colliery.

No supermarkets when this shop was around,
But trade was brisk and goods were sound.
A High Street shop, 1912.

The family of John Hudson looking smart,
Selling fruit was Hudson's art.
High Street fruit shop, 1910.

It gave them pleasure,
To make a suit to measure.
Logan the High Street hatter and
tailor, 1927. Logan, pictured on the
right, was also a well known local
historian. The Logan family arrived in
the village around 1900 from South
Shields to set up their successful
tailoring business in Easington Lane.

Colliery officials lived in this abode,
Always a clean and tidy road.
Lyons Avenue, 1936. It housed all the colliery officials, putting them in easy reach of local mines. Engines and trucks shunted the bottom half of the avenue. George Stephenson built some of his famous engines in the sheds nearby. The colliery chimney in view is that of Hetton Colliery, the first colliery in the world to mine coal from underneath limestone rock bed.

If your shoes were thin and holed,
This is where you got them soled.
Smails the cobblers, 1937. This shop stood just above the New Inn at Four Lane Ends.

Days of poverty and dole,
These poor people helped many a soul.
Poverty days in Easington Lane, 1926. Children received many a good meal at Kay's soup kitchen.

You could be sure of a helping hand,
From this good and helpful band.
Soup kitchen helpers during the 1926 strike. Without these soup kitchens a lot of folk would have starved. Local tradesmen gave produce to make the soup. Back row includes L. Larmar, T. Dickenson, Mr Brown, F. Parkinson, R. Carr, N. Gouge, Mr Stephenson. Second row includes R. Davidson, Mrs Parkinson, Mrs Loscombe, Mrs Stephenson, Mrs Brown, Mrs Laverick, J. Carr, Mrs McCabe, Mrs Sainthouse, Mrs Lamb. Front row includes L. Clish, E. Stephenson, Miss Gracie, Miss Waites, Mrs Dickenson, B. Joby, Miss Bowler, Mrs S. Vincent.

Trading with a horse and cart,
That was how he got his start.
This hardware shop traded in the village for over a hundred years until it closed in 1988.

The sun is shining what a treat,
Makes it pleasant on the street.
The High Street, 1951.

Thompsons stores showing off their staff,
Their delivery by hand cart was such a laugh.
Thompsons Red Stamp stores, 1937. This store had a delivery service by hand cart and this was pulled around the village by two of the staff. Back row, left to right: Tommy Bond, George Ayre (manager), John Harland, Elsie Tenweat, Jack Harrison. Front row: Richard Cook, John Brown, George Hall. Sadly Jack Harrison was killed by a sniper's bullet during the Second World War. What attracted customers to the Red Stamp stores was the fact that they gave red stamps with goods bought. These would be put into special books and collected over a period of time then handed in for goods or presents, usually at Christmas time.

This was the scene during the war,
Not much in the window of Pringles store.
High Street, 1944. Note the S for shelter on the corner lamp post on the right. This was pointing to a public air raid shelter in Murton Lane.

Through this gate many have departed,
With an education to get them started.
Easington Lane School, built in 1928 and still serving the village well. In 1996 it had the distinction of being voted the second best Primary school in the country.

ENL.16.

The Clock.
Its four faces view our village scene,
A time monument that should not have been.
Each chime can the mind unlock,
Memories of lads who helped save the flock.
Their names engraved on its cold sides,
The years of tears that granite hides.
Towering aloft in our High Street,
Where the boys who died used to meet.
The time it tells is of terrible war,
Of all those who died by the score.
It's years since the wars have passed,
Let our Clock be a monument to the last.

Bingo was the shout,
Now no one's about.
This hall closed its doors for the last time in 1995. The building was built as the Cosy Cinema in 1938. The first film to be shown was *Feather Your Nest* starring George Formby. It stopped showing films in the late 1950s and was turned into a bingo hall.

It was 186 High Street,
Where Boggan sold his meat.
The High Street butchers shop of J.T. Boggan, 1936. Left to right: fourteen-year-old Albert Sarah, Mary Boggan, Mr Johnson.

Elemore Vale where trees now grow,
Once miners trundled to and fro.
Elemore Vale, 1978. The large building is the old Elemore Colliery pit head baths built in 1933.
It is now used as factory units.

Built in the Lane, on route to the sea,
It travelled slowly, a sight to see.
This boat was built in the old Elemore pit head baths in 1982. It is passing Lilywhite Terrace on
its way to Sunderland docks where it was launched.

Washing drying on the line,
On Forest Estate the day is fine.
Forest Estate, 1989.

Boarded up houses on Forest estate.
Many think repairs to late.
Around 1990 this estate was demolished due to its reputation of being a hot bed of crime. A small estate was built on part of the site.

Entertainment of days long gone,
Old age pensioners every one.
Old folk entertaining in the Church Hall, 1947.

A smile on everybody's face,
The school quadrangle was the place.
An Easington Lane School junior class, 1947.

Everyone's a winner,
At this anniversary dinner.
The first anniversary Birthday party of Elemore Ladies club in the new Welfare Hall, Brickgarth, 27 March 1962. The Ladies club was formed in 1961 and is still going strong in 1997.

All hail and hearty,
Labour was their party.
Members of Easington Lane's Labour Party Women's section off to a rally in Durham City in 1945.

It was smiles galore,
In Favours store.
Originally the grocery shop of T. Holmes and sons it was sold to the firm of Favours in the late 1940s. This is the Favour staff in the 1950s. Left to right: A. Young, D. Morgan, E. Wright, F. Hutchingson, M. Oliver, M. Noble, M. Archer.

They did their work,
Without a quirk.
Women workers at the Lyons Colliery brickworks, 1920.

At milking cows she showed great skill,
Many a pail she would fill.
Local farm milk maid Annie Patton with son T. Patton, 1920.

Local farm hind of the day,
Lots of work and little pay.
J. Patton, 1920.

No one washes clothes like this today,
But in years gone this was the way.
Mrs Lily Sanderson, 1948.

Lorne Street, a queer abode,
Toilets at the other side of the road.
Susan Wharton in Lorne Street, 1954.
This street was a row of small colliery
houses that stood next to the colliery yard.
The toilets were built at the opposite side
of the main Easington Lane to Durham
road. No one knows why.

This bunker was built during the war,
When England's back was against the door.

This bunker stood in Elemore wood, and was built for the defence of our country in 1939. This photograph was taken in 1990 and shows the entrance, and the inside of the bunker. It is said to have been a wireless operation centre used by the American soldiers manning the anti-aircraft guns and searchlights at the south end of the village. Some reports say it was to be used in defence of the colliery, and another report says it was to be used by a secret army in case of invasion. The fact that it was still there in 1990, is a credit to its unknown builders.

Posing outside the club, smart and steady,
If the Germans invaded these lads were ready.
Easington Lane Home Guard, 1944.

Army cadets in khaki proud,
When England was under a big war cloud.
Easington Lane Army cadets, 1943. Left to right: J. Sanderson, T. Croft, R. McNeal, F. Howarth, J. Cullen, J. Carter.

The war years of tears and fun,
We did our bit to beat the Hun.
Victory day celebration party, Thames Street, 1945.

Two

Elemore Colliery

Towering steel structures, casting shadows on Elemore Vale,
Sunk in 1825, withstanding weather and gale.
Cradling Easington Lane, in its coal dusty arms,
Giving our village life and industrial charms.
Elemore Colliery, scenes of disaster and tears,
Wives and daughters have felt such fears.
Isabella engine house burnt to the ground in 1834,
1886, twenty-eight killed when explosion did blow.
Three men died 1943 when Duff hole caved,
Rest their souls they couldn't be saved.
Lots of others have been the toll,
But that's the price of Elemore coal.
Two redundancies have had to be faced there,
Strikes and disputes, Elemore had its share.
Pit pony Smut taken to Royal Windsor show,
Arthur Nutman the putter also did go.
Awards Wright and Cook for bravery did receive,
A trapped comrade they tried to retrieve.
Five stables housed ponies that were kept underground,
In the five seams they were to be found.
High seams and low had to be mined,
Hard working men had livings to find.
New pit head baths built in 1933,
At last from coal dust miners' wives were free.
1951 a new medical centre opened its doors,
Nurse, Sister Anderson walked its floors.
Coal is no longer drawn at Elemore's pit head,
It travels underground to Hawthorn mine instead.
Steam engines that carried coal from the mine,
Have long disappeared along with the line.
Still up the Vale miners trundled their way,
And will carry on until closing day.
Then at last Elemore had to go,
It closed its gate in nineteen seventy-four.

Words used at Elemore Colliery

Bull:	A safety device for stopping runaway tubs or small waggons.
Cat:	The coupling on a haulage rope that is fixed on to a tub or small coal waggon.
Choppy:	Hay feed for the ponies.
Chow:	A wad of tobacco.
Chummings:	Empty coal tubs or small wagons.
Cow:	A safety device for stopping coal tubs running backwards.
Crib:	A container for holding feed for ponies underground.
Dog:	A large nail or spike for keeping railway in position.
Donkey:	A narrow piece of belting used for pulling conveyor belts together.
Galloway:	A pit pony.
Head tree:	A small temporary wood roof support.
Hedgehog:	Loose strands of wire on a steel haulage rope.
Kist:	The meeting place of a district underground.
Limbers:	A set of shafts used by ponies for pulling coal tubs.
Mell:	A large hammer.
Monkey:	A device for fixing hand drilling machines to wood props to keep them steady.
Nog:	A stand of wood support chocks.
Plate:	A shaped piece of iron for joining together an arch girder.
Plates:	Two small lengths of waggon way rail lines.
Rapper:	A system of signalling using large hammers. Later using electrical hand pullers.
Scalloper:	An air pick using compressed air.
Shieldie:	A cover to put on hand held oil or electric lamps. This was to stop the glare hurting the following man's eyes.
Worm:	Part of a hand drilling machine.

The heaps where coal was picked during the strike,
They carried it home on barrow or bike.

Elemore slag heaps as they were in 1984. It was during the great miners' strike of 1984 that most of the men and boys of Easington Lane would come to these slag heaps to dig for waste coal during the year long dispute. It was the only way to get fuel for themselves and their families.

Elemore Colliery our place of work,
Hard toil no place to shirk.

This is where many spent their working life,
But work was hard and full of strife.
Early view of Elemore Colliery, 1900.

These Elemore fitters were skilled and sound,
They kept the pit wheels turning round.
In the pit yard, 1949. Left to right: L. Thwaites, T. Pattinson, R. Tate, K. Guy, A. Munro, S. Swan.

Miners of time long gone,
Hard workers every one.
Elemore miners, 1922.

Steam engines that carried coal from the mine,
Have long disappeared along with the line.
This engine carried coal from Elemore around 1900. It was built at the Hetton Lyons sheds and was known as the Hetton Engine. It now stands in Beamish Museum.

Nineteen forty the war at its height,
Elemore coals helped win the fight.
At that time, using picks and shovels, ponies and tubs, the colliery was producing over 1,000 tons of coal per day.

Ready with their oil lamps lit,
Boys waiting to go down the pit.

Fourteen-year-old boys at Elemore Colliery, 1902. Boys of fourteen, some still in short trousers, would have no trouble starting work at local collieries. Very quickly, without specialised training, they would be soon skilled in the many jobs done by the young lads of the day. Boys would become experts at coupling, twinning, dreging and driving. They would also be skilled in landing the set, cocking the rapper, filling the dish and placing the muckle. Their minds would be full of things like flat sheets, limbers, shieldies, knocky off bars and chummings. Quickly they would learn to yoke a gallaway and ride a galloway. Words like worms, hedgehogs, donkeys, dogs and frogs, took on a totally new meaning. So at the tender age of sixteen, having had two years work in the pit behind them, boys were half way to becoming skilled miners. As they worked their way up the work's ladder new words and jobs would emerge; the likes of putting, filling, roll offs, scallopers and strip packers. There would be gummers, scufflers, back over turns and double turns. It was a world of strange words and jobs that will be remembered by many, but sadly with the collieries closed and the coalfield gone those jobs and words are being lost for ever.

Elemore Vale looking towards the pit,
Today the scene's changed a bit.
Elemore Vale, 1939.

School boy memories back of the mind,
These young boys had a living to find.
A group of young miners, Elemore Colliery, 1916. Back, eft to right: George Nattras, Tommy Whiteman, Fred Dover. Front: Harry Stevenson, Tommy Kavanach.

Start of their shift with lighting of oil,
In the bowels of the earth these men would sweat and toil.
Elemore miners, 1920.

Their job was hewing coal,
Underground like the mole.
Elemore Colliery miners, 1928.

Being a blacksmith was their chosen grade,
Elemore Colliery was where they learned their trade.
Elemore blacksmith shops, 1928.

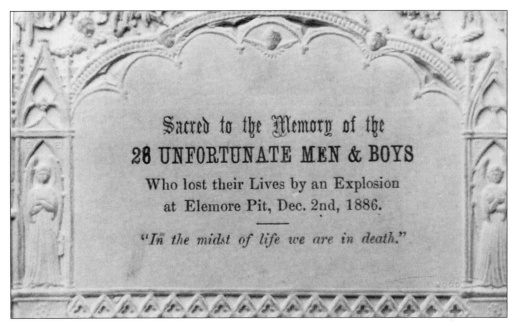

Sacred to the Memory of the
28 UNFORTUNATE MEN & BOYS
Who lost their Lives by an Explosion
at Elemore Pit, Dec. 2nd, 1886.

"In the midst of life we are in death."

Our village was racked in pain and sorrow,
For those who died there was no tomorrow.
Elemore explosion, 2 December 1886.

MINERS'
WELFARE FUND
ELEMORE COLLIERY
PITHEAD BATHS

THESE BATHS ERECTED BY THE
MINERS WELFARE COMMITTEE
IN PURSUANCE OF THE
MINING INDUSTRY ACT 1926
WERE OPENED AND HANDED
OVER TO THE TRUSTEES
ON THE 2ND DEC 1933

To come home nice and clean,
Had always been the miners' dream.

Boys doing a man's job well,
What they thought no one can tell.
Elemore boy miners, J. Craig, C. Gouge, P. Hardy, 1922.

Posing near the pit cage,
Then underground to make a wage.
Left to right: C. Rodgers, J. Kent. A tragic story about J. Kent occurred after he left the pit and joined the army. In 1941 when returning home on leave he arrived at Durham to find that all roads were blocked out of the city due to heavy falls of snow. With no transport available he decided to walk home to Easington Lane. He got as far as Pittington then became trapped in a very large snow drift and sadly that is where he died.

Colliery officials of the local pit,
They knew their work and did their bit.
Colliery officials, 1908.

Elemore Colliery was where they worked,
A place where many dangers lurked.
Local miners, 1930s.

At the show he was led around,
But his life was spent underground.
Elemore pit pony with handler, J. Clough on the right, 1948.

From the King and Queen a pat and a smile,
As handler and pit pony Smut did it in style.
Handler Arthur Nutman and pit pony Smut at the Royal Windsor show, 1939.

*They marched to the brass band
beat,*
Proudly through a Hetton street.
Elemore miners' banner being
paraded through Hetton in the
May Day parade. Bill Barry is
carrying the banner, Bob
Merrington is on the right,
Jimmy Flyn behind and Bobby
Telford is the other carrier.

Standing in front of the banner proud,
Elemore they shouted clear and loud.
Mrs Christine Wilson at the centenary Gala, 1983.

Banner lifted at the ready,
Then off they go very steady.
Parading the banner around the village before going to the Gala at Durham City was the usual practice in most colliery villages. Here it is in 1983.

To the miners Gala they proudly marched,
When they arrived they were really parched.
The last time Elemore Colliery banner was seen at the Durham Gala, 1983. Left to right: R. Telford, N. Lee, Band master of Easington Prize Band (name unknown), I. Riley.

Music ready, homeward bound,
They would thrill the crowds with their sound.
Elemore banner at the Centenary Gala, 1983.

In a Hetton chapel stands Elemore banner high in all its glory,
A tribute to the workmen who created the Elemore Colliery story.

The last shift emerges into the light,
To save the pit they have lost the fight.
The last working shift to leave Elemore Colliery, 1 February 1974.

Norman Lee the watchman, the last man around,
Soon the shafts will be filled, and all levelled to the ground.
Elemore Colliery closed in 1974.

Three
Religion

Easington Lane in its early days,
Was a mining place set in its ways.
Then the ranters came and preached their book,
Just a few turned out to take a look.
Those few must have sown the seeds,
Because chapels were built to serve their needs.
Three in the Brickgarth were soon on the go,
With a church in the High Street to make it four.
The Salvation Army were next to arrive,
Their church on Pembertons Bank made it five.
The Apostolics soon proved they could mix,
By building in Lyons Lane church number six.
Then the catholics for their place in heaven,
At the south of the village church number seven.
Lastly the Spiritualists entered the religious gate
In Derwent Street with chapel number eight.

Our Lyons church has served us well,
If stones could talk, tales it would tell.
Lyons Parish church was built in 1886 at a cost of £4,000. The first vicar was Richard Goodhudd. A new roof was put on the church in 1985 at the cost of £40,000, ten times more than the cost of the original building.

Here many couples have been matched,
Children baptised, and the old despatched.
Lyons Parish church, 1942.

The vicarage, the vicars abode,
Not far from the church just down the road.
It was built around the early 1900s and turned into a nursing home in 1988.

Being built in the rectory ground,
A home to keep old folk safe and sound.
The old rectory being converted into a nursing home in 1988.

In our village religion has its place,
On Sundays you would go in your satin and lace.
Easington Lane Primitive Methodist chapel in the Brickgarth as it was in 1900. Built at a cost of £1,800 in the late 1880s, it served our village well for many years. A report of a chapel tea in 1890 reads: 165 adults at 6d each, 40 at 3d each, 135 children at 1d each; total cost of feeding 340 persons, £5 3s 9d.

The Primitive Methodists closed at last,
It served us well in the past.
This chapel was pulled down in 1977 and a smaller chapel built on the site. This was opened Saturday 29 August 1981.

Once marriages were made to last,
This is a certificate of years long past.
Marriage certificate, 1902.

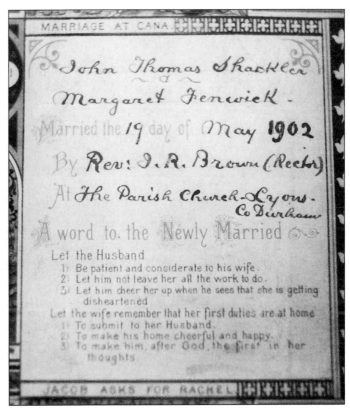

The church of the Salvation Army looking grand,
The people who attended are a joyful band.
The church of the Salvation Army was built in Elemore Lane in 1967.

The Boys Brigade looking smart,
Even the elders played their part.

Chapel members with the Boys Brigade outside the Independent chapel, 1922. The gentleman third from the left, second row from the front, was Mr Charles Grey a miner at Elemore Colliery, who in 1945 became the Labour Member of Parliament for Durham and held the position of Controller of the Royal Household in the Labour Government.

Camping in the Yorkshire Dales,
Carrying water in gallon pails.

The Boys Own youth club in the Yorkshire Dales, 1947. The Boys Own was a youth club run by the Independent Methodist chapel in the late 1940s and early '50s. With Arthur (Monte) Grey at the helm it did a grand job looking after the youth of the village.

Camping with the Boys Own in nineteen forty-seven,
For these children it was seventh heaven.

Apostolics posing in the street,
For the children it must have been a treat.

Members of the Apostolic church at the back of their ramshackle church at the top of Lyons Lane in 1925. The building on the right is their church. The building on the left is the Travellers Rest public house. The old lodging house, where beds could be had for one penny a night, is second on the left.

In this chapel they spent many an hour,
The mediums there had lots of power.
The Spiritualists chapel in Derwent Street was built in the early 1930s and pulled down in the late 1970s.

There's always a welcome at the door,
No one could ask for more.
Apostolic church in Elemore Lane. This building was once the catholic school. It was taken over by the Apostolic church in 1987 when they sold their church in Murton Lane.

It served our village when times were rough,
The preachers there knew their stuff.
Wesleyan chapel in the Brickgarth, built in 1827, demolished in 1950.

Our Church Hall looking grand,
No graffiti or vandals hand.

The Church Hall as it was in 1936. The buildings started off as a school in around 1870. In 1928 the church took it over as their hall when the new school was built at the top end of the village. It was then used for many social occasions that went on in the village. It is best remembered for the Saturday night dances that were held there for many years, where for six pence you could dance the night away to the sweet music of the boys club dance band.

Young schoolboys poured petrol on the floor,
And up it went with a roar.

The burning down of the Church Hall caused by young vandals in 1987. The culprits were never caught and the fire still remains a mystery.

After-math of the blaze,
And many problems did it raise.

It stood like an ugly sore,
As vandals destroyed it more and more.

Before they started with the wall,
Get the slates off was the call.
Dismantling started in June 1988.

The machines move relentlessly on,
And soon it will be all gone.

All that is left of our village hall,
Rubble, girders, and a wall.

Our hall's gone, more the shame,
Youth and vandals must share the blame.

After the fire permission was sought,
To build the flats of Tower Court.

These flats were built on the site of the old Church Hall in the early 1990s. The scaffolding around the Clock Tower was for repairs to the Clock in 1995.

Four
Brickgarth Memories

Colliery houses row after row and noises from the mine,
That's how I remember the Brickgarth before nineteen thirty-nine.
Oil lit store carts rumbling home, having sold their wares,
Children playing street games, children have no cares.
Sound of the pit boot as miners hurry to and fro,
Monday, pos sticks thumping washing white as snow.
And clearly 'away away' from the gardens came the cry,
As stocks of racing pigeons went flying by.
Who can forget on window ledges cooling like cart wheels,
The sight of lovely stotty cakes for appetising meals.
From the miners hall the sound of the trumpet and the hymns,
The Salvation Army trying to save the sins.
Also holding meetings there the Good Templers, after banning drink,
Many signed the pledge, with a naughty wink.
From the Davy Lamp, Nags Head and Gardeners beer was sold,
And also Martin Bank to save your gold.
At the trunks and the old mill boys played with glee,
After ten many a fight you would see.
Halls for fish and chips, bread and cakes Dover baked,
Down in the gambling school many a pound staked.
The Pot shop and Collwils yard were known to most,
Four places of worship the Brickgarth could boast.
We all can remember Mrs Harland sitting at the step,
Tot and Phil Collett always full of pep,
Cock Robinson who lost his legs on the pit line,
Hills, Charltons, Tempests all worked down the mine.
Also Purvis, Bowman, Turnbull, Wharton and lots of others too,
Good folk we have mentioned just a few.
Lads and Lasses bowling 'oily gigs' racing down the street,
And others playing deliver, hear their running feet.
Jack shine the maggy you could hear some one shout,
In a chalk ring marbles being knocked about.
In the welfare hall sound of the dominoes being shuffled,
From the pit engine whistle, sounds slightly muffled.
Where colliery houses once stood a council estate has grown,
Gone forever places this verse has shown.
Now the place has changed, but the name still remains,
But pleasant happy memories the mind still retains.

Washing jam jars for their pay,
These people earned six pence a day.

These workers from the 1920s are from Colwill's Marine yard which was situated at the west end of the Brickgarth. It was owned and run by one armed Billy Colwill shown on the left of the picture. Colwill's yard as it was known locally was in fact only a scrap yard and survived for many years.

A schoolboy and his dog in the yard,
Growing up during the war was very hard.
Brian Hardy in the Brickgarth, 1941.

The old age pensioners at the start of their outing,
Lots of laughter, joy and shouting.

This was the first organised outing for the aged of our village in 1947. It was the start of the over sixties club who meet in the welfare hall, or as it is now called the Community Centre, situated in the centre of the Brickgarth. Here are the pensioners waiting for the outing buses. The welfare hall is in the foreground and the Independent chapel at the back.

Out for a walk,
And a talk.
Two Brickgarth men, Enoch Evans and Robert Wharton.

The Brickgarth on a sunny day,
For the children time for play.
A Brickgarth scene, 1902. The building on the right is the Old Elemore Union Hall. The large building in the centre is the Primitive Methodist chapel while the tall building, far right, is the Co-operative store.

Dressed for the show and ready to go,
Store show horse Damsel, made his owners glow.
Damsel was owned by the Co-operative store and won many prizes in the local flower shows. Matthew Stephenson is at the horses head with other Co-op staff. The photograph was taken at the Co-operative stables just off the Brickgarth in Bradley Terrace, 1912.

The Co-operative store committee of 1920,
They stocked their shelves with good and plenty.
In the 1920s and '30s the Co-op was the largest shop in the village and was centred in the middle of the Brickgarth. It had its own stables to serve the many horses it used in their splendid delivery service around the village and surrounding area. The Co-op also built its own tennis courts for the staff, to keep them fit and healthy. It closed in the 1980s but by that time it was a shadow of its former self after serving the village as the Easington Lane and South Hetton Co-operative Society for nearly a hundred years – from the 1880s to the 1980s.

Earth midden toilets and tin baths,
Not much money but plenty laughs.
Colliery houses in the Brickgarth, 1935.

Standing on a Brickgarth step,
Looking happy, full of pep.
Etty Wharton, a minery wife, 1935.

None of these lads could drive,
But make believe kept them alive.
Lads pose on a motor bike and side car in the
Brickgarth in 1938. R. Wharton is in the
driving seat, Joe Gordon is in the side car,
Reay Wharton is behind the driver and Tom
Whitfield is in the background. Reay Wharton
spent the Second World War in a German
prison of war camp. Sadly he died just after
being released due to eating contaminated
corn beef.

70

Five

Pubs

The Pub Crawl

At the top of the Lane stands the Three Tuns Inn,
A place where you might meet some of your kin.
Same side of the road hundred yards down the street,
The Commercial Inn, a place where friends like to meet.
Move to the Free Gardeners Arms, all Tudor in style,
Enter the bar, try a pint, stop a while.
Across the road an Inn once stood, Albion was its name,
Not many will remember, that spot is not the same.
Move on, turn left to Elemore, snuggled in the Vale,
The Three Tuns Inn, grand little pub sells good ale.
Continue up the road a while, its only a little walk,
There you will see the golf club, have a little talk.
Next in line comes the Bonnie Pit Lad, always plenty of chatter,
If you fancy dominoes, in there you will hear them clatter.
Along the Brickgarth now we go, the Davy Lamp comes on show,
Pint or two in there, then steady as you go.
Further along the Nags Head stood, a queer place I believe,
From the pit men would go, no wages wives receive.
Now back on the High Street, the Grapes Inn we enter,
Darts being played, double top, twenty-five or dead centre.
Then go into the Workmen's club, just across the street,
The doorman and fruit machines will be there to greet.
On our way, pass by the church, memories now on view,
The Cross House Inn, closed down now sadness for a few.
A few yards further the Lord Seaham Inn, plenty music here,
In the room young folk dancing, records loud and clear.
Cross over to Lyons Lane, look with all your might,
You will not see the Black Horse, houses on that site.
Also gone the Travellers Rest, but memories still remain,
Please don't day dream here, we must move on again.
Make haste the Cricket Club we must see, hurry down the road,
Sit down and have a drink, it is our last abode.

They decorated this building with loving care,
Folk passing by would stand and stare.

The Cross House Inn all decorated up for the local flower show and carnival, 1928. It was the custom in those days for all the public houses to dress up their premises for the show, and prizes would be given to the winner. Sadly this custom, along with the carnivals and flower shows, died out over the years.

Go to the top of Lyons Lane, and look with all your might,
You will not see the Black Horse, houses on this site.

Black Horse, 1909. This public house closed in 1936, the last landlord was R. MacNeil.

Fashion of the day,
For work or play.
Landlord and family of the Bonnie Pit Lad, 1890. The pub was built in 1848 and the first owner was Anthony Brydon a colliery manager or viewer as he was called in those days.

The beer flowed freely in this drinking house,
Not a place to take your spouse.
A group of customers in the back yard of the Bonnie Pit Lad, 1890. Easington Lane had fifteen drinking houses in 1890, all doing a roaring trade.

The Commercial Hotel was greatly respected,
Good ale was what folk expected.
Commercial Hotel, 1905. This public house was built in the 1840s and was first called the Joiners Arms. It later became the Commercial Hotel, then the Commercial Inn, then just the Commercial. It also acquired the nickname Deuchers. In 1992 its name was officially changed to Deuchers. In 1996 it closed and in early October of that year vandals broke into the building and set it on fire burning its interior to a shell.

Just above the Four Lane Ends this pub stood,
Where all the beer was drawn from the wood.
The Abyssinia Hotel, 1916. This in its early days was called the Tyneside Inn.

Pull the beer,
It gives good cheer.
Inside the Bonnie Pit Lad, 1952. Left to right: A. Donnison, J. Fairhurst, Tommy Heslop.

The Free Gardeners Arms, all Tudor style,
Try a pint, stop a while.
Known locally as the Long Pull, this pub was built in 1825, and is the village's oldest public house. The Tudor fronting was put on in 1928 when the building got a face lift. It was given the name the Long Pull in the days of horse and carts. The blacksmith's shop was next door and traders bringing their horses to be shod would have to travel up Pembertons Bank, hence when they arrived they would say its been a long pull as they slipped into the Gardeners for a pint, and those words stuck.

While watching the show,
The drink did flow.
Inside the Workmen's club, 1980. Left to right: Norman March, Annie March, Ruth Sanderson, Jack Sanderson.

Show a leg was the shout,
As the ladies danced about.
The ladies box doing their stuff entertaining members in 1980. Left to right: L. Lyons, J. Hall, G. Pretty, J. Ellis.

Six
Sport and Pastimes

Victory Day Handicap.
Welfare Back to Welfare via Lyons Colliery, $2\frac{1}{2}$ miles.

Bill Taylor started the race away,
Nineteen Forty Five on Victory day.
Straight away Isaac Croft set the pace,
One of the favourites for the race.
Others settled in behind,
Pace too hot some to find.
Tom Tempest was lying third,
And Jos Wharton's breathing was heard.
Jack Corner and Tommy Whittle very handy,
Not far behind Barty and little Sandy.
Norman Hunter was moving through the field,
When to the roadside Isaac Croft keeled.
Knees went off he did tell,
When he was going well.
Passing the Lyons class was showing,
Now Tom Armstrong was surely slowing.
And now Norman Green was fading fast,
It was doubtful if some would last.
Round the corner past the New Inn,
It was eyesight who would win.
Up the road they all sped,
But Jos Wharton looked half dead.
Pembertons Bank the pace did quicken,
Then Tommy Brass' wind began to thicken.
Round William's Corner well in the lead,
Came Tommy Tempest running at full speed.
Then Jackie Corner came in sight,
His legs like lead, face ashen white.
Into third place Tommy Whittle staggered,
Very tired with face all haggard.
Boxer Walton and others now in view,
Boxer looked as if he'd had a few.
Jos Wharton and Tom Armstrong did not get places,
They both finished looking like hospital cases.
Few will forget that entertaining race,
In happy memories it has its place.

On the field they gave their all,
With the bat and the ball.
Lyons cricket team, 1901.

Their aim was to knock a six,
They soon had the opposition in a fix.
Lyons Wednesday cricket team, 1911.

Foot running was their game,
First to the tape was their aim.
A group of runners, 1920. Running was very popular in Easington Lane and the surrounding area at that time.

In days gone the craze was bikes,
They saved your feet from those long hikes.
Easington Lane's first bicycle club, standing in front of the Bonnie Pit Lad, 1890.

In the football strip of the day,
Our church team could skilfully play.
Lyons parish church football team, 1900. The goalkeeper in the centre with the cap is
W. Taylor.

Turning professional was the loving dream,
Of all the boys in this football team.
Easington Lane School football team, 1920. The two trainers are Bun Robson (left) and
Thomas Latimer (right).

Best schoolboy football team around,
They played other teams into the ground.
Easington Lane School football team, 1935-36. Back row, left to right: Mr J. Hall, W. Story, R. Weirs, C. Nicholson, Mr Mason, J. Hudson, R. Nutman, M. Cullen, Mr Ficklin. Middle row: T. Williamson, W. Richardson, J. Ladler, H. Dodds, F. Hope. Front row: M. Walton, G. Groves.

England cap upon his head,
A schoolboy wizard it was said.
Timmy Williamson played for England schoolboys against Ireland in 1937. He is shaking hands with headmaster Eric Mason in the quadrangle of Easington Lane School.

There was no charge on the gate,
But to spectators their team was great.
On the Flatts ground Easington Lane, 1949.

On the field they didn't do bad,
But when they lost they were really sad.
Easington Lane School football team, 1947-48. Back row, left to right: W. Heslop, A. Liddle, J. Nicholson, W. Stoker, R. Philips, F. Wright. Front row: K. Hall, J. Eliott, J. Petty, R. Wiseman, J. Dance.

Lyons boys club football team,
Scoring goals was their dream.
J. Telford, centre with ball, scored 69 goals that season, 1948.

The day the Durham Amateur Cup was won,
They held a party, lots of fun.
A football dinner to celebrate Easington Lane winning the Durham Amateur Cup in 1951.

They were feared home and away,
Ball control was their style of play.

By supporters they were proudly hailed,
Home or away they rarely failed.

Easington Lane football team on the Flatts ground, 1950. Note the old Brickgarth in the background.

Easington Lane football team of the 1950s.

For enthusiasm they were hard to beat,
To see them play was a treat.
Lyons Parish church school team, 1927. Back row: C. Wilson, Revd Laws, T. Brecon, Percy Barcus (Elemore Colliery manager), W. Lowery, C. Waters, S. Illis, J. Cresswell, T. Moore, J. Hall. Front row: P. Collet, R. Donkin, J. Hutson, J. James, S. Cresswell. The team are in front of the vicarage. Revd Laws was one of the longest serving vicars at Lyons parish church and was a very popular man.

They played the game when times were rough,
But these boys club lads knew their stuff.
Lyons boys club football team, 1939. Note the old Brickgarth in the background. The policeman in the centre is PC Wandless who was one of the boys club leaders.

The jolly boys was this teams name,
On the field they enjoyed the game.
Easington Lane Workmen's club, Jolly Boys football team, 1947. Back row: J. Wild, A. Derbyshire, D. Morgan, J. Loscome, J. Telford, W. Richardson. Front row: T. Purvis, Timmy Williamson, G. Wigham, E. Charlton, J. Murphy, F. Young. The name of the young boy is not known.

The school team of years long gone,
But happy memories for everyone.
The team of 1954. Back row: Mr Wilkes, Mr Soulsby. Middle row: R. Adey, T. Nut, T. Nelson, M. Crooks, J. Cormack, Ian Patterson. Front row: Mr J. Steel, -?-, B. Usher, D. Hudson, W. Taylor, R. Nixon, Mr Kelly. Brian Usher went on to play for Sunderland and the England under 21 team.

For this school camp, these boys were glad,
It was the only holiday they ever had.
Easington Lane School at camp in the Yorkshire Dales, 1938.

Breast stroke or crawl,
Was the aim for all.
A group of children from Easington Lane and the surrounding area, members of the Lyons boys club, 1939. This pool was the Lyons Colliery pit pond, converted into a swimming pool by the leaders and members of the boys club, and was in use for many years. No one was ever drowned or hurt in all the time it was used. Today the area is now landscaped into parkland and lakes, but for the older generation of our village it still holds happy memories of open air swimming days of long ago.

In the garden safe and sound,
As she swings up from the ground.
Christine Sanderson on a back garden swing in 1956. We can see back Pembertons Bank, with Cross Row and back Lyons Lane.

Joker, Jester, and the Queen, posing in the street,
Carnival time in our village, was an annual treat.
Carnival day in June 1934. Dressed up for the
carnival parade: Ante Johnson (the jester),
John George Walton (Queen), Pat Hardy
(King). These carnivals were once an eagerly
waited for event in the village. They were
usually held once a year in June with many folk
dressed up for the occasion. There would be
sports for the children, and sporting
competitions between the pubs including;
quoits matches, tug of war and darts. The
festivities would go on for a week and would
end with a grand parade through the village
with bands and clowns adding to the carnival
atmosphere.

Proudly marching banner high,
In competitions they caught the judges eye.
The Fusiliers jazz band marching through the village in the late 1960s.

*Marching through our
village always full of pep,
All the little children,
never out of step.*
Easington Lane
Buccaneers jazz band,
1964. Left to right:
Lorna Simpson, Walter
Ayre, Linda Wilson,
Rosalind Metcalf.

*Jazz bands
competing in the
Flatts,
With twirling sticks
and waving hats.*
Jazz bands in
competition on the
Flatts ground in
1965. The 1960s
were the jazz band
era in Easington
Lane. There were
two bands in the
village, the
Fusiliers and the
Buccaneers and
there was great
rivalry between the
two.

Posing in their Sunday best,
These men had pigeons that could stand the test.
Easington Lane's first pigeon club was formed
in 1905 and is still going strong today in
1997. Two members, Brass and Bruce, won
the Up North Combine Pigeon race two years
running with the same pigeon, a record which
still standing today. The races were from
Mons in 1921 and Troys in 1922.
Membership today stands around fifty and
most of the lofts are centred around the
Elemore Vale garden allotments and the
Brickgarth gardens.

Miners have always enjoyed their sport and play,
This was a typical pigeon loft of the day.
Jack and Ruth Sanderson, 1953.

A pigeon fancier taking stock,
Handling two of his flock.
Jack Sanderson and Jack Price at the pigeon
loft, 1952.

Husband at work during the race,
So the wife took his place.
Mrs Sanderson waiting for the birds to return
from a race, 1953.

Their hobby was keeping stock,
Here they are with their bantam cock.
Poultry fanciers with their show bird in the garden at Lorne Street in 1931 before heading off to the local show where no doubt they hoped to win first prize.

The gamekeepers would the forest roam,
These cottages were their home.

Gamekeepers cottages, Elemore Wood, 1938. These cottages were close to the Big Hill in Elemore Wood. This hill was a favourite picnic area on Easter Monday for the folk of Easington Lane for many years until losing its popularity in the 1970s. Let us now take a nostalgic trip back to the Easters of our childhood, a day at the Big Hill. Families would make the trek for the annual picnic, and time has not dimmed the magic of those days. Walk up Elemore Vale, past Elemore Colliery, turn left at the colliery manager's house, and up to Thompsons farm, and over the style. Past the big black water tank that stood high on stone pillars. To us children it was just a big tank for holding water, but in reality it was a very simple and unique water system for the manager's house. Water from the mine was pumped some nine hundred yards to the tank. As this was above the height of the house, gravity would pull the water to the taps. When the water level in the tank dropped, it would set off a bell in the colliery pump house, thus starting the pump to fill the tank. Moving on we follow the path over the fields, skirt Elemore wood, over the little bridge, and the Big Hill fanned out before your eyes, and so would start a never to be forgotten picnic. Boiled eggs, jam sandwiches or fat and bread and a bottle of water. When it was your turn to drink the water it was usually full of floating bread crumbs. Then there was running, jumping, swinging on trees and rolling down the hill. At last, tired and scruffy, we would wend our way home, another Easter Monday over. Today the road still wends it way to the Big Hill, but alas the colliery is gone forever. The Big Tank is also just a memory. One can still stand on the little bridge and look, but all will be quiet; and the weather, it seems a little colder these days. For today's transistorized kids the Big Hill may seem a bit tame, but for yesterday's children it was full of happy memories.

Our village as it used to be,
The year was 1953.

We have seen religion from the start,
In the pub crawl we have taken part.
We have visited the Brickgarth in memories eye,
Remembered the village hall as the years fly bye.
Viewed the colliery scene with its dust and noise,
Along with the miners, men and boys.
Sporting moments seen at a glance,
Our village carnivals with their song and dance.
The war years our village gave its all,
When everyone rallied to the call.
We hope this journey through our village street,
Has given you all a nostalgic treat.